LOW FANCY

LOW FANCY

CATRIONA STRANG

~

Scores by François Houle

ECW PRESS

Copyright © Catriona Strang 1993

Parts of this work in earlier versions have appeared or are forthcoming in *West Coast Line*, *Raddle Moon*, *Lyric&*, *O·blēk*, and *Big Allis*. The author would like to thank Jeff Derksen, François Houle, Lisa Robertson, Nancy Shaw, Colin Smith, and Melissa Wolsak.

The general editor of ECW PRESS poetry books is Bruce Whiteman.

CANADIAN CATALOGUING IN PUBLICATION DATA

Strang, Catriona
  Low fancy

Poems.
ISBN 1-55022-197-3

I. Title

PS8587.T73L79 1993   C811'.54   C93-094245-0
PR9199.3.S87L79 1993

Published with the assistance of The Canada Council and the Ontario Arts Council.

Design and imaging by ECW Type & Art, Oakville, Ontario.

Distributed by General Distribution Services, 30 Lesmill Road, Toronto, Ontario M3B 2T6.

Published by ECW PRESS, 1980 Queen Street East, Toronto, Ontario M4L 1J2.

for LISA ROBERTSON & CHRISTINE STEWART

Though the medieval way is still thought good enough, what is to prevent some modern Girl from rising from the Couch of a Girl as modern, with something new in her Mind?

— Djuna Barnes

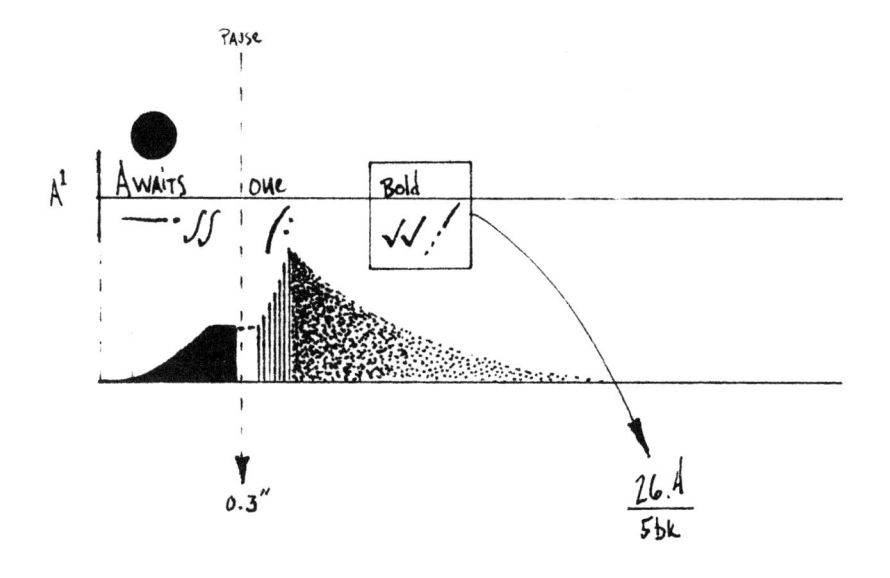

Avert sighs, ignore decorum:
   our stops redeem us
whose florid queen's a kiss.
   We tail libation's cult
though time proffers its necessary insult —
   our token penance.

Let abundance read it
Eve, I am consenting.
Very jocund, um, prod it
God — EAT! I invent us.
New and gaudier forms
a venial mood — on my knees
for your breast — serenade her
(and redden temporarily);
new florid face I am
a renovated flower.

Rise you! Of this hell it's
torpor or high malice;
extol it all to us or
curse us — I've all there is.
SOUL is the beneficial
key; oh such lick bravo! I
received it to pore — "EM."
Venus is sick at our stalling tempers:
"Nostrils, pectorals, is
reficiate ardour for them."

Imagine my SURPRISE at finding my own intervention glossed over in a marginal note, a conjectural emendation of three distinct hands and an ungrammatical linger spiked with flickering brawl, as striking as a rotten tapestry's green parrot or the blackening tooth of a mouth whose tongue knows no frontiers. But this MYSTERY's only one of the earliest corrosives in a popular confusion bitten by patterns of repetition, and a gathering intensity that SUCCUMBS to the easy charms of the remote. When was my mood ever untranslatable?

But not susurrant.
Trip us is carmine: "aha, contrary"
or: means flower at the spine
full of all and can or
call it tenerous, curious
delect at us (useless):
It's a key.

Said it hums to a durity
(fuck!) or able, it, ridge of a glacier
is brumal, as fur, ready *as it is*
to pour, or — improbable — Ignite! is
colour, ire at pallor.

Edging a rise or
extol all means of his
absence in it; tell us carmine, delect
and do — I sang rind.

To begin now is to accept that horrified FASCINATION associated with scarcely legible fragments and infamous lacunae; even as their parchment is snuffed to become imbrued with fervid intention, and the perpetually unpredictable call of an Imaginary Jerusalem (which only grows more pronounced despite the proliferation of variants not always for the better). Thereafter all that's certain is a meaning that's obscene. Yet a perversely subtle intensity SPRAWLS here and there over mouthfuls whose voluptuous disputation rakes calumny up into a particularly suggestive struggle — one which rings injudicious in the common estimation.

For all ease lent
it trods a gay tryst while folly cavorts
nor can it promote odd fires and due riot
not when mauled and plainly stung —
we're lit.

I'm vernant, knocked over, the, uh
fruit you pulsed for times renewed
and interminable rigid dolts.
Spate. Swank like lilacs
though a lewd calm might cap
this fulgid verging.

So forget ardour —
anxious choler swipes my high tread
once the fulcrum's veined.

Lean edges bear a more than aural
advantage: deduce *this* indecorous
to be subjected — it's facile.
Certain qualms deign to manage, rove
so dab it, or (tenderly) arise.

Read trapped, I I am virgal
as if cunning tore under
rid the face of us, though
easily you *can* dance here.
It's as no appearance, not us
not them: undone, and let clear out.

Nor must revise it
from high iced nips
save to *kiss* it:
let's be juvenile
with flowering gaud . . .

True, she's adept. Lagan of eyes
clear and nitid her nub does
knock my cant pliable — *shit*
one mood's grit empties days.
Up top it's hot, sweet, and I'm malleable.

According to the unanimous testimony of every contemporary, a striking feature of our well-established violations is their perpetrator's adherence to a shifting and private technique in the face of indifferent (if urgent) stimulation. Accorded neither authority nor influence, the wandering scheme was calculated to DISLODGE a dedication to veneration, yet to disrupt the exchange that had already ensnared my lucid minority. Although the ensuing discourse often had the guise of an amatory affair, it was most often fed by a generally CHURLISH contempt cloaking a rank threat that could never be altogether prohibited. Characterized by a bitter antisacerdotalism and a certain love of SPEED, the wanderers' constant vigilance produced a dangerous abundance of interceptions, and pigmented the imagination of an entire century.

I am, I am. Strident, prating
yammering a verge in so
dent or tear can
rid you (fact is)
if knocked as apparent.
Or let not one squeal for a clear route.

Name us a reverse cut —
the frond frets hiemal
saves a cease; it
lets you vein
congenial. All voice
a more licit "I am" — in a debt's urge.

To air goes my lit times
simulates none: very
trusting; a vital mist
knows its tenor key
of culled, loquent visage.

Try hands.

Fast and nefarious, ambled and
vacantly erred through avarice
pared past pain fit into
a prodigious dream, temperamentally sung.
Don't doubt this aversion
mediates an untrammeled
cue; we'll vitiate
cautious contemplation.

Understand that my anonymous striplings harmonized neither reason nor ingenious introspection, but with a SPURIOUS illumination stumbled contrarily through an overwrought century whose villainous orthodoxy rooted, and unquestionably lingers in an over translated version.

Said like regained matter set in
the aped pall of a deep protest
(paired to cream indignity's
tang) — this muscular presumption
backs qualms adequately
and numbs
our volatile ease.

Next night I'll bop
and suss this dizzy leave.

Nudge a turn day in, day out
or deem aspiration doused her.
Name who lies a turgid burn or
appalls an ease —
that's virtue fucked
all lusts annulled
in a poxy lisp of
venomous debilitation.

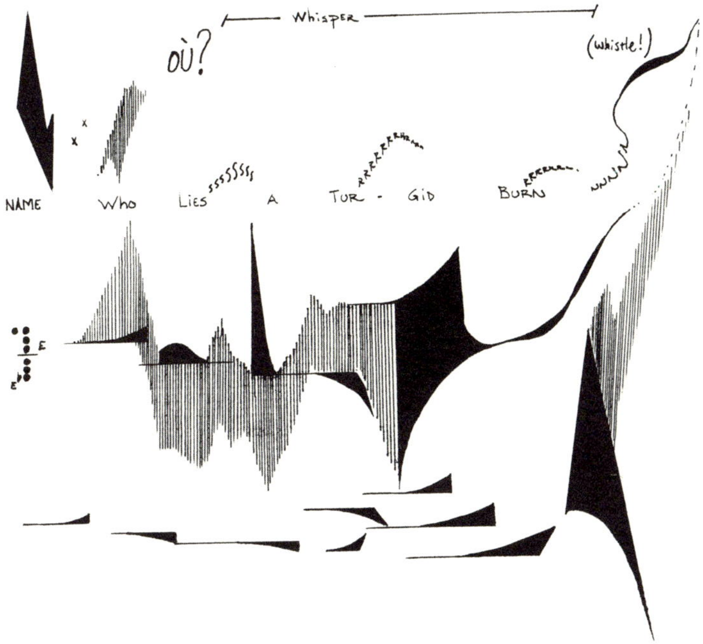
Whisper
OÙ?
(whistle!)
NAME
Who
LIES
A
TUR -
GID
BURN
E
E♭

As potent as licentious is
exquisite — it's yours
and expedient to bite at; it
rips scurfy cerebral repletion.
Scathing, I
won't sleep;
this pliant surmounts
the inaudible probe.

Creep or tear enough
potential might procure this
feast-up, or at least cull
interminable modesties — lechery tossed
aggrieves moderation most
(as a certain ignominy
best attests).

If so, latitude quickens a thickly
furtive key no loud venom
can curate; for an ostensibly illicit
it pours back a cohort's exit — no more
to burst this gravest manner
than to recede as consort
and tune a nicked pair.

Tempt us best of
jocund urgings; our mood's
gaudy with
love's juveniles.

Can't sick the ominous
feel that dulls sight
audibly, modulates
an intrusive call.

Of lurid totter I am
more genially ardent. All this
newest, novice love is riven
quoted peril.

YOUR
PROMISE
DEPORTS
SIMPLICITY

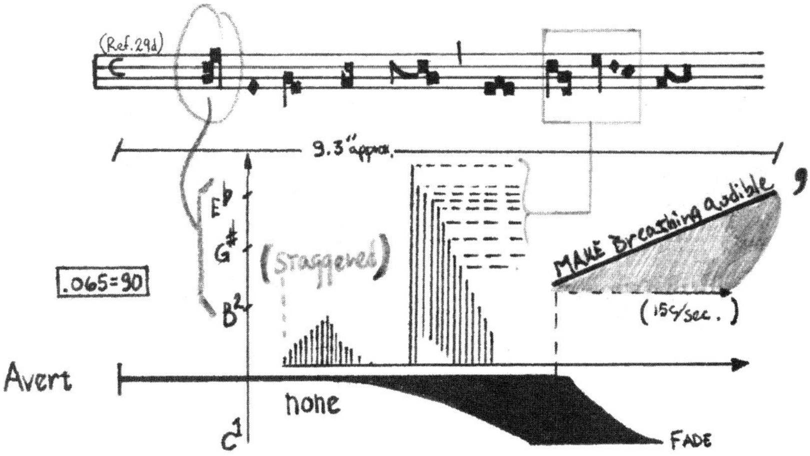
(Ref.29d)
9.3" approx.
.065=90
E♭
G♯
B2
C1
(Staggered)
MAKE Breathing audible
(15c/sec.)
Avert
none
FADE

Just as no appearance routes
a temporary pretense clearly ribald
but quickly sickened; so ornamental fury
busts its pretty florid tune.

> *Avert none. Our silver can*
> *it cannot dull all gory ends.*

In example: *never* rise
dap fabulous proponents over
feeble hackles, or bustle names — it irks
all equitable yearnings
to rope so lewd a turn.

Am, or a query invents
this ludicrous verging, come in
despite its venal scenes.
Who can unpleat all our ribbing stunts?

> *Avert none. Our silver can*
> *it cannot dull all gory ends.*

Capriciously, I intend to deliver these abstemious cravings with as UNCOUTH a proliferation of unfathomables as can flower under the tyrannous heel of a paraphrase, although my historicity is a somewhat irregular example of its species culled from an intimate familiarity with labourious and partly indecipherable rehabilitations. Such defects are no more troubling than the duly commensurate ordination of an INGENIOUS guess; in either case any omission is altogether emphatic. Governed by this corrupt singularity of motive, our dispute's proportions wander outrageously through passages embedded with sinister understatement, bawling out the presence of a distinct IRRITATION it can neither carry nor obscure.

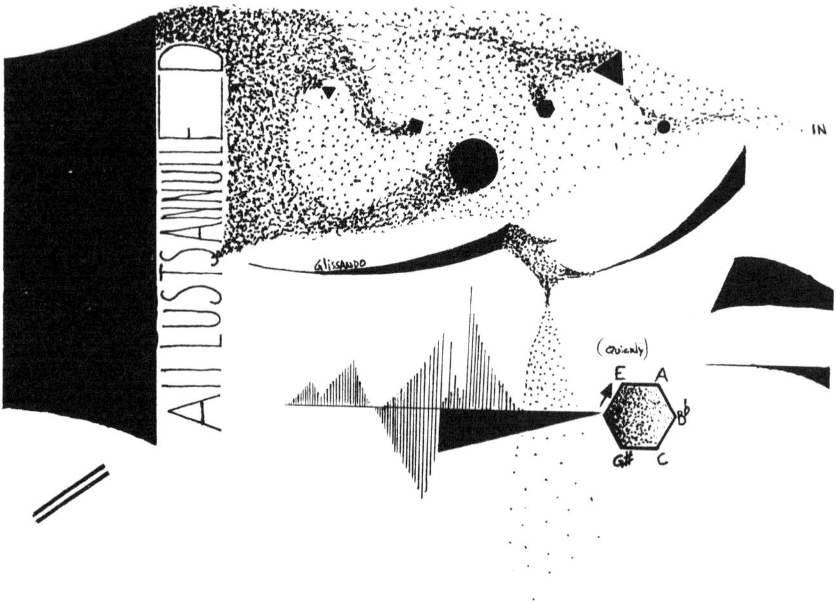
ALLLUSTSANNULLED
IN
GLISSANDO
(Quietly)
E
A
B♭
C
G#

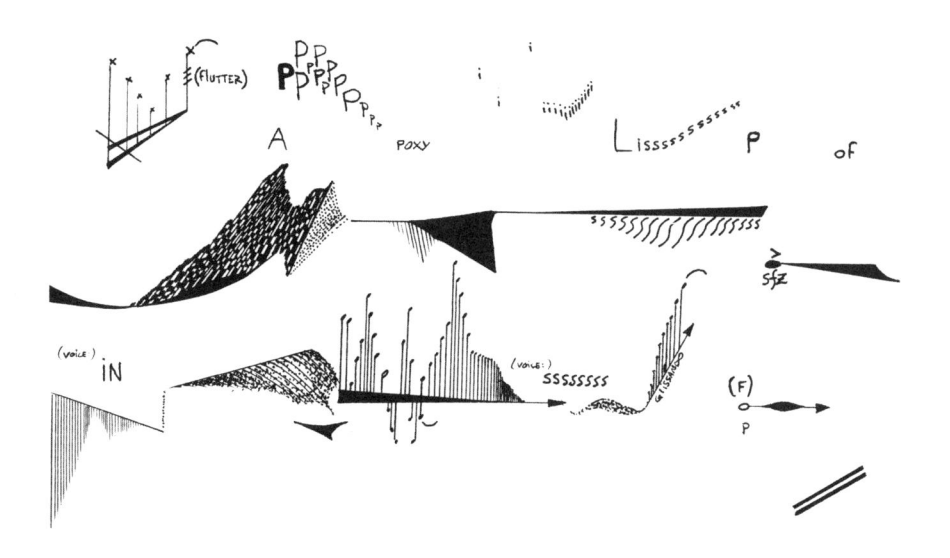

Leg it lightly;
memory's an inquest
whose tonic cumbles ethics:
addled, ambulant, and glorious
a becoming bonus.

I'd dispone *any* minimum
and cite supine eras
to prime my dear hocks
so, script, console us: "kiss, sit."
Dignity's done.

Christ's dice, it's true.
My dick can rarely, rarely care;
it's as caring as a nun's habit.
Ubiquitous.

It rants an unveiled script
whose visceral ply inveigles
use: "do more, come more" — I'll roam
and bulge a fulminant leave.

Convene none, the dare's
out: numb bones esteem no virtue
nor escape a secondary quip
(as absolutely no one said).
Daring risks a potent dig
and mirrors all numerous
familiars — if my prize vice
incurs a novice intuition.

Tear up, I've
panned it: a dull chase
might test us to a grateful
rerun or caulked queue — there's no
cavorting in your veins.

I'd strep a resplendent search
or tread some promoted riot
but, odd, I can't — there's no
fulcrum to the well-inked day.
I'm all hymns and glass.

In any case, this much is clear: my inexplicable interjection had sewn a field of new and taxing possibilities whose exaggerations were mutual; henceforth, as intermediary I would simply DISPORT there with a sincere and violent conviction.

Respond, sweet — charity's
dubious; my quivers
solicit the same quick, not
your own cloistered neck.
It nicks censure
cuckolds a useful query.

I go all saucy at qualms
but come ploring and you'll
leave; it's transient
if richly summed: no astute
grabs it all.

Omit a must, you'd
etch culled despair
and carp a most delicate vent;
your toothy era nets
an apt senectitude, or
resets an intender's series.

It's a perturbing luxe
our studied vex detains;
as lascivious as sugar
a tender, roused invention.

No stray veer humps
labour's proper tactic —
our vital's patched; it
macerates a carnal cure.
All bloody stops inhabit us, deter
a picked guard or, no, I'm
numb — our minute familiar's
a moribund tussle.

It's a perturbing luxe
our studied vex detains;
as lascivious as sugar
a tender, roused invention.

Promise: comfort
kill me, o deport me
don't

Even in a culture almost visibly acquiring an embellished apostasy, the utter dismissal of Rome's enticing safety valves could be said to constitute a genuine act of aggression against the old excesses. It was more than indifference. Impelled by a conscious rejection, our recurrent conflict BRISTLED through the centuries, taking to cover in unfavourable times and rioting at others. It was fostered in fields, houses, and workshops, and from now on only the most spectacular ASPECTS of subsequent developments diverted common attention.

                Attest:
                Our conquest's over
our time rendered dumb
by tremendous dicing, dying
        purile supplication
                damn misery
        and perennial sadness.
We duck the rest;
        it's a numb infernal voice.
Our salve's a ruse
        turgid and eternal.

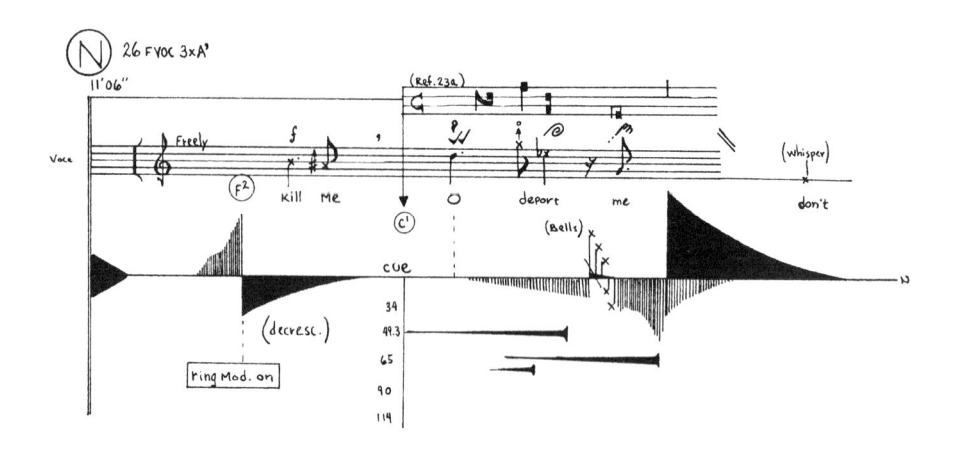

In unison, love's
puling — a vulnerary perk
in a molting, lurid mode;
it'll quench terror.

The dumbest pulse
turfs empire — we'll quit
these feeble men or bask
our amenable inch
in deepest, frigid draughts.

I'm out! Misery's eaten
my utmost — I'll sip
at admired wrecks and decline
destiny's itch.

Said I'd tilt *any* tale
if fronds ram us and
subtle foliage — thyme's
vernant. Come, best
and game me
quite chord our fit.

In patient gaming we've grazed
a cunning murmur. It rives us
a low curse, is festive's
vent, and tussles like
temper's suss — as sure
as your ratty tempest.

A̲nd still a culprit fails to emerge. In fact, everything appertaining to my unpronounceable invariably VANISHES, as though swathed in a secret register accessible only through the utterance of some VACUOUS curse, or conjured up like a fake and distant relic, a splintered production either indifferent or actively hostile to the fawning cravings of our brutal new ethic. But solely on the basis of the machinations of this alien creed, who could mistrust so persuasive a testimony, delivered in such a plausible tongue? And yet the SWINDLE remains, venerated with an intention so vile even accidental addictions yielded. "We cannot undo it," my hooligans declare.

Late nape's lit
from this rammel-full;
I'd muck an amusing bust
thigh dicks and grab mine: so nab
my chosen, fitting career.

Sick my suss can end
or all out neck
our facet's solo; who fugues
my proxy fatal or collars
a blandest inept — my cordy dolour?
I dump what cock amends, or said "no love."

As if they're ill, knocked
or dormant — so sure
is a lip's maul, brave as marrow.
My digs turf quite a net: see
all gaud this taunting reception.

Still, I'd dump you all
so movingly as to lash
gesture's civil hunt
and quaff a vile endeavour.

Me, I'm subreption's height.

O Cupid, concede us
love's cohort
hope, who solicits
innovation's ego, mentor
to my turbulent hocks.

Hiss lascivious fill;
this verdant veer
is adamant — thyme
roses, lilies
allude ominous melodies.

Meanwhile, there is scant indication of the heady idleness that displaced harsh medieval RANKLING with a whole new contrition; although required by the patient habit of the popular, this mysterious thread resurfaces rarely. It hums most often beneath restorations of profane dissimilarity, PUNGENT in the violence of their confession, and always indicative of the excommunicative boot poised directly above our sinking ground. Hidden still, the censorious BITE of these shrouded alterations can never be overlooked; within their listing traces ranks a boldly driven note:

N3x96 (slow)

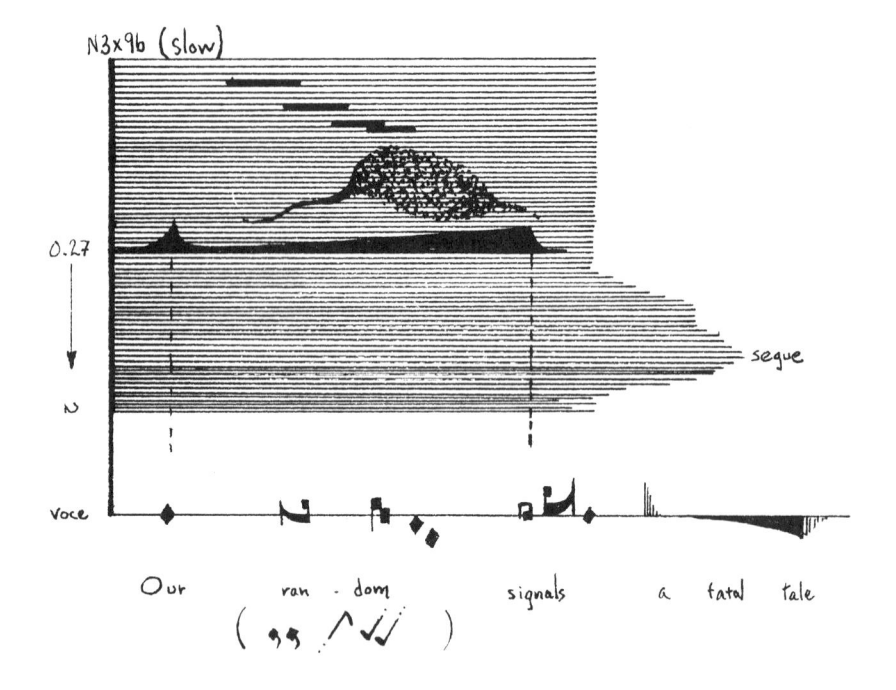

0.27
↓
2

seque

Voce

Our   ran - dom   signals   a   fatal   tale

Hire us
lucid; I'm
finesse undue.

Our random
signals a fatal
tale, and cools
a lusty queue —

Some volage runs a vivid rile
if equality's dialogue
sits diligent, so kiss
the amended censor — I alter none.
Petter, your strops hack
for vulgar commerce
or impart nascent
amateurs. They'll forset
a precarious volt
and pry us admired.

Puler! I cannot salve
lucre's test — nor in parting
solve her redolent odour.

An ominous feel
tilts protest's sly
pour: can't torque enough
sure deep.

Venal domicile
cumbrous and gaudy!
Even bellies vent
or I *am* perished.

In light of my lewdsters' GRIEVOUS thrashing at the hands of a pretty popular kind of war, it seems important to emphasize that they were neither PESTILENT nor insane. Compelled by enjoyment, they dreamt up their own splendour, and there is no need to reiterate that their methods opted for potency. My rabble did not TRIFLE within the greasy constraints of their vocabulary. Their voracious blasphemies irritated an established snare to the horizons of its diablerie; it is my own devious duty to strive towards an emulation of such eminent heresy.

Quest no mirable pair
ineffable men — do I
ram rage at a ton's treat?
Perhaps my fine siren's hammer
is too expansive; it riots
an incubate satire, exercises
a larval voice and fawning hand. It
out-cites, or abates.
She's a Christian tart who rumps:
"Tune us, do us, and conserve our abject host — I burst dignity's rise."

● Thigh   dicks   and   grab   mine

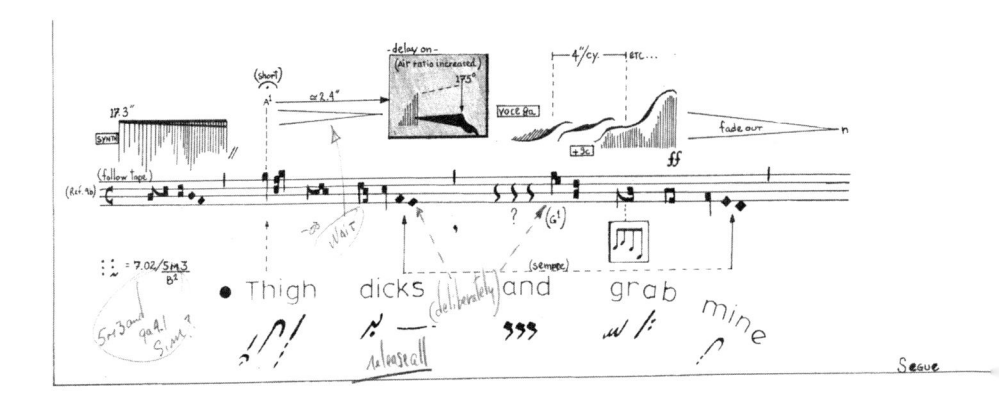

Segue

Virtue eyes us
and trims pernicious ravel.

Come contingent; you're a pressed pair —
it's a bribe as obsequious
as no paid stare possessed
and not quite dared: a verbal wreck.
Sit, tidbit, salutes are said:
        our vast pottering
evacuates simpers, or sums
        a maximum squeem.

Or come sit in enamoured regions;
I'll appall all dear protests.
Our indignant tantrums
sever a query's meek peril
and muck back loot's calm:
        presume us oscular
we sustain a choice neck
        celebrate the night air.

Avert sighs, ignore decorum:
   our stops redeem us
whose florid queen's a kiss.
   We tail libation's cult
though time proffers its necessary insult —
   our token pennant.